K. E. BENNETT

Coastal Orange County California Travel Guide

Explore Coastal OC Like A Local - Enjoy The California Riviera

Copyright © 2023 by K. E. Bennett

All rights reserved. No part of this publication may be reproduced, stored or transmitted in any form or by any means, electronic, mechanical, photocopying, recording, scanning, or otherwise without written permission from the publisher. It is illegal to copy this book, post it to a website, or distribute it by any other means without permission.

K. E. Bennett asserts the moral right to be identified as the author of this work.

K. E. Bennett has no responsibility for the persistence or accuracy of URLs for external or third-party Internet Websites referred to in this publication and does not guarantee that any content on such Websites is, or will remain, accurate or appropriate.

Designations used by companies to distinguish their products are often claimed as trademarks. All brand names and product names used in this book and on its cover are trade names, service marks, trademarks and registered trademarks of their respective owners. The publishers and the book are not associated with any product or vendor mentioned in this book. None of the companies referenced within the book have endorsed the book.

First edition

This book was professionally typeset on Reedsy.
Find out more at reedsy.com

This little book is dedicated to all those who have supported, guided, and held me up in my life as I worked through my various challenges and opportunities. Your love, dedication, and loyalty to me continue to leave me in awe and gratitude. I am so blessed.

Contents

1	Introduction	1
2	Getting Here, Planning Your Trip, and What to Bring	4
3	Iconic Ways to Get Your Trip Started	11
4	Orange County's Best Beaches	19
5	Fabulous Shopping Destinations	29
6	Dining Out	36
7	Great Hikes and Walks	43
8	Family Friendly Experiences	48
9	Cultural Experiences	54
10	Non-Hiking Adventures	60
11	Outdoor Bars With A View	70
12	Conclusion	76
13	Resources	77
	About the Author	80

1

Introduction

Congratulations, and I'm so glad you're joining me in learning about and loving all the things that make coastal Orange County such a great place to experience! You've come to the right place if you want to learn about beautiful, fun, and adventurous experiences that you can enjoy on your trip to Southern California.

I wrote this book to help people like you enjoy an experience that is beyond what you can imagine. Orange County is home to some of the most beautiful and iconic and unique locations in the country. Whether you've been living in Southern California for years or you're visiting for the first time, this book will turn you on to some hidden gems that we locals enjoy over and over again.

It's always a little risky when you travel to a new place - even if it's right down the road! Thirty miles away can feel like "long distance" or inaccessible to our daily lives when you live in Southern California. The traffic can be unpredictable, and with an hour or two of drive time, it's worth it to really know what is worth doing in coastal Orange County. If you're traveling from out of town, that's even more of a gamble! Trip planning can leave you with lots of questions like: Is my hotel in the right location? Which beaches should I go to? Which restaurants are really worthy of their Yelp reviews? Do I listen to the concierge at the hotel? What are the MUST sees?

I wrote this book to help you with all of that, and by the time we're done, my hope is that you will have fallen in love with coastal Orange County just as much as I have! There is still one really important question remaining - who am I, and why should you listen to my advice? Well, without going too deep into detail, I'm a Southern California native who has lived in coastal Orange County for the last 20+ years, and I know my way around the "pretty" places. I cut my teeth at Chez Panisse in Berkeley, Spago in West LA, Harvel's in Santa Monica for a little live blues music, and lots of time at the Hollywood Bowl and the Greek Theater. Spending time in the San Francisco Bay Area and Los Angeles allowed me access to some of the best restaurants in the country, and I know a good meal when I find one. That being said, I don't like to overpay for things, and I have curated recommendations that I feel are well worth their price. I wouldn't send you to a restaurant that has average food just because it relies on its location on the water to keep it afloat. The restaurants you'll find in this book are great, the beaches are beautiful and/or iconic, and the activities are among those most enjoyed by the locals.

I'm a teacher by trade and I live just a mile from the water in Huntington Beach. I frequently enjoy happy hour with my

INTRODUCTION

friends at the locations I recommend, and the restaurants are among those I select to celebrate someone's important events such as birthdays or anniversaries. I've personally experienced nearly everything in this book, and I would return to nearly all of them (exceptions being those designed specifically for children). But who knows, someday I might be a grandma and I'll be back to those places too!

One of my strongest desires is to give back to society in a positive way by utilizing my unique skills and perspectives to make people's lives better. I hope you use this book as a way to enjoy your time in Orange County and that you get to know it a little better than you do by watching reality TV and/or shows like The Real Housewives, The OC, The Hills, or Selling OC!

If you're ready, let's get to it!

2

Getting Here, Planning Your Trip, and What to Bring

Getting to Orange County, California: There are so many ways to get to coastal Orange County, but generally speaking, you're going to end up on the 405 Freeway. You'll use your phone to navigate once you arrive, but I've outlined some airport information with pros and cons about each to help you decide what's best for you. I hope this helps in getting you into and out of OC in a way that is comfortable and efficient for you.

My order of preference for airports is:

1. John Wayne Airport (SNA)
2. Long Beach Airport (LGB)
3. Los Angeles International Airport (LAX)

Additional Airport Information:

John Wayne Airport (SNA)

- John Wayne Airport is the preferred airport for visiting Orange County. I would choose to fly in and out of SNA 100% of the time if I could always get the flights I wanted. It sits very close to the heart of Orange County and is a very functional mid-sized airport which is pleasant to fly into and out of. If you can, book your flight into and out of SNA. The only limitations may occur with the timing of flights since no take-offs or landings are allowed at SNA between the hours of 11pm and 7am.

Los Angeles International Airport (LAX)

- LAX is a much larger airport than both John Wayne and Long Beach, and it includes a much busier experience and a longer drive to OC. With the longer drive comes a bigger Uber/Lyft or car fee. If you are renting a car, it's not as much of an issue. If the flight to LAX is much cheaper than the one to SNA, decide based on your budget and the time of day. If you're going to be sitting in rush hour traffic on your arrival, SNA might be worth the extra money.

Long Beach Airport (LGB)

- Long Beach is also a nice little airport, however, being that it is much smaller than the other two airports, it will have more limited choices in terms of flight times. That being said, I particularly enjoy flying in and out of Long Beach because it is an older, very small airport, and the look of the airport has been maintained to keep the "old Los Angeles" architectural feel. It's a treat and feels like a step back in time even though its technology is modern.

Burbank and Ontario Airports are also in the Southern California area, but I would avoid them if possible since they are a much longer drive from Orange County. You could use either of these airports, however, just factor in that much longer drive. And while we're talking about drives, Southern California traffic can be challenging, and that long drive, while seemingly only an extra hour, could be as long as 2-3 hours. Choose carefully.

Planning Your Trip:

You'll need to secure flights, your hotel or Airbnb, and a rental car. Other than that, pretty much anything you could need or want will be available to you.

We've discussed airports, let's spend a little time on hotels. Southern California, if you have never been, is full of cities that are directly adjacent to each other with no way to differentiate between them other than a sign that might say "Now Entering: __" or "Welcome To: ___". Even though the Orange County that you see on TV is all gorgeous beaches, restaurants, hotels, and people, it's a big city place with big city amenities and big city challenges. So it's important that you choose well as you're booking your accommodations. Public transportation is not as strong as we would like, so having a rental car will be important if you want to do much away from where you're staying. It's

GETTING HERE, PLANNING YOUR TRIP, AND WHAT TO BRING

also important to choose a good location for your stay.

Looking at the map below from www.enjoyorangecounty.com, you can see that Orange County is a fairly large area. This guide, and its activities, are focused to the west of the west-most freeway. Looking at the map, that's either the 405 freeway, the 73 freeway (toll required), and furthest south, the 5 freeway. Generally speaking, I recommend you look for accommodations in this general area, that is, west of these freeways. If budget isn't an issue, then you may be looking at any number of waterfront hotels on the beaches in OC.

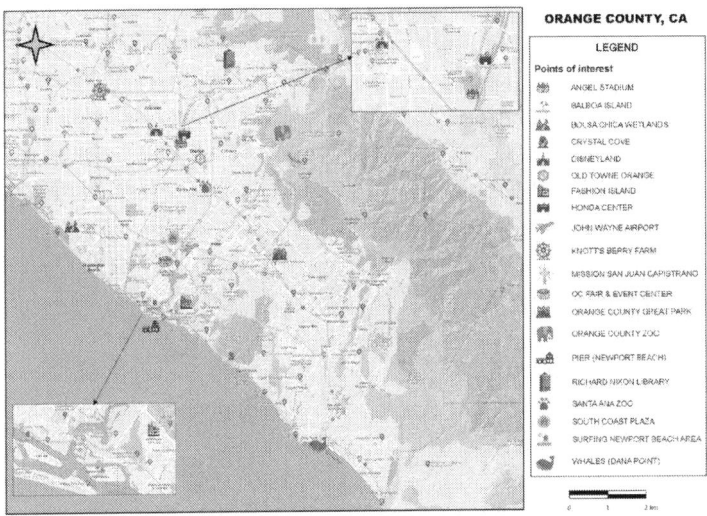

A note about choosing your accommodation locations. When you book your place to stay, keep in mind that location will matter to your experience. As with all things real estate -

location, location, location! If you are looking for the ultimate luxury experience, you may find yourself in South Orange County at the Montage or the Ritz. If you're looking for more things to do directly out your front door, the hotels on the beach in Huntington Beach might be more your speed. And if you're not going to be staying oceanfront, choosing something more centrally located might make the most sense.

Rental cars are another consideration that I won't spend much time on except to say that you will most likely want a car. Southern California is a car-based city, and without one, things can be more difficult. If you're choosing a resort right at the beach and you only intend to spend time at the resort and at the beach, you might do fine with rideshare services like Uber and Lyft. If you're planning on taking advantage of many of the activities in this guide, a car would be a better option. Rental cars are available as needed with reservations at the airports and through the other car rental options available. Check online for your favorite option.

Weather:

No matter what time of year you come to Orange County, the weather will be mild. The hottest month, August, averages a high of 84 with an average low of 64. It's early September as I write this, and I walked outside last night in shorts and a light jacket. In the coldest months, December and January, the highs range between 68 - 69 and lows are in the mid 40's. It is important to note that 68 degrees in the summer is REALLY different from 68 degrees in the winter.

GETTING HERE, PLANNING YOUR TRIP, AND WHAT TO BRING

I can't tell you the number of tourists I've seen walking down the Huntington Beach pier in December or January wearing shorts and flip flops, and they look really cold! Don't be uncomfortable. While the weather is mild, and it may seem like shorts weather compared to where you're from, I recommend always having a light jacket, sweater, or sweatshirt in the evening on all but the hottest evenings. During the day, take your guide by the season and the surrounding days' temperatures.

Because there is so little rain in Southern California, the ground retains a lot of heat, so milder temperatures can feel warmer. Conversely, even though the air temperature may be 65 in the winter, the ground may be much colder, making you feel cold. And of course, the air temperature is always modulated by the temperature of the Pacific Ocean which ranges from the high 50's to as high as 70 degrees at the peak of summer. And one final note about Santa Ana winds. These types of winds are off-shore winds which bring warmer temperatures, sometimes catching you by surprise with a 90 degree day. Not much to know about them, but it might be worth packing a set of clothes that can help you be more comfortable in a little unseasonably warm weather.

Interestingly, I have a friend who visits frequently from Las Vegas to get out of the 110 degree heat. She arrives and promptly puts on a sweatshirt because it is SO much cooler here that it feels cold to her. So keep that in mind when you're packing.

What To Bring:

Generally speaking, Orange County is a pretty casual place. You can get by with "beach casual" clothing just about anywhere except the higher end restaurants. And nicer business casual is fine for those places as well.

If you're going to Disneyland you're going to be doing a lot of walking - bring good shoes. If you're going out to nice dinners, bring nicer clothes. Bring a bathing suit if you're going to swim or beach. I always recommend an SPF rash guard if you're going to be swimming, paddleboarding, or just hanging out for a long time at the beach. A packable hat is always good, and don't forget plenty of sunscreen.

There are lots of packing list suggestions on the internet, so I'll leave that up to you, but keep in mind that there will be a Target, CVS, or a Walmart not too far away, so don't sweat it if you forget a little something.

3

Iconic Ways to Get Your Trip Started

Top Places to Visit and Ways to Start Your Trip

Each of the items in this chapter require very little of you - just show up and enjoy. They are an easy and enjoyable way to spend a few hours, or more should you choose to add a meal or some power shopping. I have done all of these, and continue to do them, because they are special little journeys to sprinkle into everyday life.

Pacific Coast Highway Drive:

They say you can get your kicks on Route 66, and I have! But I'm partial to Pacific Coast Highway and all the great things you can find along the way. Start your trip by driving up and down PCH from Seal Beach to the north, and to downtown San Clemente in the south. This will take you about 2-3 hours, depending on traffic and the time of day. This is a fabulous way to just "lay eyes on" some of the awesome places laid out in this guide and it will help you get a feel for which places will be most appealing to you. It will also help you plan your stay if you don't already have everything planned out. When I need a little jolt of inspiration or just a break from my day to day, you can find me doing this drive with the music cranked up loud. It just feels good. If you have a convertible, put the top down - here's the perfect opportunity to soak up some sun and get the "lay of the land".

Sunset along Pacific Coast Highway, Huntington Beach. By Johnathon Cook-Fisher.
https://www.flickr.com/photos/jcookfisher/11617339773

Huntington Beach Pier and Downtown Huntington Beach:

What's not to like about Surf City, USA! If you just want to get out and stretch your legs a bit, the Huntington Beach Pier and downtown HB are a good choice and also an iconic place to visit. I recommend you walk up and down the length of the pier, and then walk up Main Street until the shops begin to thin out and/or you lose interest. There are lots of interesting bars, restaurants, and shops to explore, and you can find deals on surf apparel right there at the corner of PCH and Main Street. The Sugar Shack has been around longer than I can remember, and is a locals favorite for breakfast. You could also stop at Sandbar and get an enormous frozen margarita! You might want to share unless you're good at stopping brain-freeze! Tuesday nights is the farmer's market downtown so that's always a fun time to go.

It's nice and cool under the Huntington Beach Pier in the heat of the summer. Photo by K. E. Bennett.

Laguna Main Beach and Downtown Laguna Beach:

Laguna used to be an artists colony and it retains some of that artistic feel with its art galleries and unique shops. Laguna's Main Beach is on the cover of this book, and it is a gorgeous place to spend some time. There are people playing basketball, sometimes volleyball, swimming, walking the short boardwalk, or just hanging out on the grass. There are restaurants, ice cream shops, bars, etc. You could easily spend the better part of an afternoon and evening strolling through the streets and enjoying the beach scene. Laguna is a must-visit on your trip to coastal Orange County.

View from the gazebo overlooking Laguna Beach. Photo by K. E. Bennett.

Balboa Island and the Balboa Island Ferry:

Balboa Island is a tiny island in Newport Beach, and visiting the island is a lovely way to spend an afternoon. I enjoy Balboa Island in the morning too and sometimes visit to walk the exterior of the island and look at the gorgeous houses. It can be nice to get there before the little town wakes up and everyone converges to visit this idyllic little downtown area. Walking around and shopping are lovely in Balboa, but as I mentioned before, I think the real appeal is in looking at the houses. They are just spectacular to look at and dream about. You could try a morning walk around Balboa and downtown, get your steps in, and enjoy the morning air with some serious "architectural eye candy".

COASTAL ORANGE COUNTY CALIFORNIA TRAVEL GUIDE

*Bike ride onto the Balboa Island Ferry, then enjoy the view!
Photo by K. E. Bennett.*

San Clemente Pier and Downtown San Clemente

I personally think downtown San Clemente is some of the cutest shopping you'll see. It reminds me of Carmel, but with a Southern California surf vibe. We can call it "Carmel South" if you'd like! You can stroll up and down Avenida Del Mar and enjoy the shops and restaurants and maybe catch the farmer's market on Sunday mornings. Afternoons in San Clemente are my favorite - one of the reasons being the weather. Sometimes it takes until the afternoon for the sun to break through the marine layer, but it's worth the wait! The San Clemente Beach Trail is also a very enjoyable experience which can end with a nice breakfast on the pier if you'd like. That's my personal favorite way to experience the beach trail and pier.

Seal Beach Pier and Downtown Seal Beach

Seal Beach is another cute little beach town with lots of shops and restaurants. Seal Beach feels very "old-school" and is one of my favorite places to visit when I'm not feeling like the bigger crowds and fancier places. Seal Beach has quite a few good eateries including Walt's Wharf which you'll find on my list of Top 10 restaurants. A Cold Stone Ice Creamery, directly across the street from the pier, is a big crowd-pleaser as are the tacos, hot dogs, coffee shops, and bars.

Seal Beach Pier. By Traveler100 - Own work, CC BY-SA 3.0, https://commons.wikimedia.org/w/index.php?curid=12847294

4

Orange County's Best Beaches

Each of these beaches has their own appeal and charm. Some are enormous expanses of beach, and some are tiny little beaches - this guide will help you decide where you'd like to go. I would be remiss if I didn't mention that rip currents are very common at the beaches in Southern California. Given that, it is risky to swim where there is no lifeguard. If you plan to swim and/or your kids plan to swim, please do so in front of one of the many manned lifeguard towers. Staying safe while having fun is the idea.

Crystal Cove State Beach

Crystal Cove is my personal favorite public beach. The water is clear, the sand is pretty, it's big enough to go for a nice walk yet it feels like a special and secluded place. The beach itself is quite big but the way it is nestled into its little cove makes it feel intimate. There are also vintage cottages available to rent, and they make it look and feel even more special. The Beachcomber Restaurant sits at the bottom of the hill and right on the beach, making it a spectacular place to grab a burger or a cocktail. The Shake Shack is at the top of the hill, and on weekends, the line of cars to get food or a shake extends onto PCH.

Huntington Beach, Dog Beach, and Bolsa Chica State Beach

Huntington Beach and the attached beaches are huge! The expanse extends from Warner Avenue just south of Sunset Beach to the north, and all the way south to the Santa Ana River and Newport Beach to the south. There are so many places you can go along this beach, and if you want to say you went to the beach in Huntington Beach, this is it! Most sections include paid parking, restroom facilities, and in some cases, restaurants on the beach. Be sure to check out Sea Legs on the Beach (near Warner Avenue) if you feel like a drink or snack or some live music with your toes in the sand.

Being closer to the pier is certainly a good choice, but, given the huge expanse of beach in this area of Orange County, you could choose other locations with lifeguards that might be just as pleasant with fewer crowds.

In the middle of this expanse, and north of the pier, is an area called dog beach, where people can run their dogs. It's always fun to watch the dogs jump, run, and play at the beach and in the ocean.

Of course Huntington Beach is known for its surfing, and you can surf on both sides of the pier and in other locations of these beaches where the waves are good. Follow the people in wetsuits! There are lots of lessons available too!

You can fish, swim, birdwatch, or build a fire in one of the first come, first served fire rings. If you want a fire ring for an evening bonfire, be prepared to "pit sit," that is, secure a fire pit early in the day and have someone stay there to ensure it is still available in the evening. Yes, we have to "pit sit" if we want a fire pit at night - there is no reservation system.

Couple walks along the path above Huntington Dog Beach with the Huntington Beach Pier in the distance. Photo by K. E. Bennett

Seal Beach

Seal Beach is a lovely little beach. It is one of my favorite beaches because it is smaller, the downtown area is quite casual, and it seems like a nicer choice for kids. There are restrooms that are easily walkable, a little play area for kids, and of course, the pier, the beach, the waves, the tacos, the ice cream… need I say more?

A pretty winter morning on the Seal Beach Pier. Photo by M. Mulcahy.

Salt Creek Beach

Salt Creek Beach is another smaller beach south of the Montage Hotel in South Laguna. It is kind of out of the way, which is one of its many appeals, in addition to the fact that it has excellent surfing, body surfing, and some tide pools. Some of the great things about Salt Creek are that it is tucked away and kind of private-feeling yet it has amenities like restrooms, basic food, and some equipment rentals.

Salt Creek Beach after the kelp has washed ashore. https://commons.wikimedia.org/wiki/File:Salt_Creek_Beach_%2811319645364%29.jpg by Jukka.

Main Beach (Laguna Beach)

Main Beach is another of my favorite beaches! Typically the crowds are not as big on the sand, but there can be plenty of people in town, on the boardwalk, and hanging out at the beach. If you play basketball and want to get in on a pick-up game, this would be your spot.

Laguna's Main Beach on a quiet Saturday morning. Photo by K. E. Bennett.

Doheny State Beach

Doheny State Beach is another popular beach near the harbor in Dana Point. It has an expanse of sand, fire pits, and a lively crowd of people. There is surfing, volleyball, kayaking, paddleboarding, as well as restrooms and showers. Doheny Beach is another iconic beach in Orange County and could be a great choice for your time at the beach. It can be a nice choice for children as well since the waves are protected by the Dana Point Harbor, making it an ideal place to learn how to surf or just enjoy the water.

Newport Beach Beaches and The Wedge

There are multiple beaches within Newport Beach, but I wanted to highlight a few of them

Newport Beach Municipal Beach is located directly south of the Newport Beach pier and extends down to Golden Beach, the Balboa Pier and Balboa Beach. At the far southern end of Balboa Beach is The Wedge. To me, these beaches are known for their proximity to the bike path that begins near E Street, and extends slightly past the Newport Beach pier. This is one of my favorite bike paths, and there are people who like to extend their ride and take their ride all the way up to Huntington Beach and back. The bike path doesn't extend all the way to HB, but there is a path a lot of the way.

The Wedge is worth visiting just to watch the waves and see the athletes. The Wedge, because of its location, has the possibility of 30 foot waves which can be spectacular to witness. If you're a surfer or bodysurfer, please make sure you do a little research before you brave The Wedge - it can be treacherous. The athletes are so talented and brave, and I love to watch their skill and expertise, particularly with the larger waves.

Body surfer braves The Wedge in Newport Beach. https://commons.wikimedia.org/wiki/File:The_Wedge.jpg by Kiffer Creveling

Corona del Mar and Little Corona del Mar Beaches

The beautiful beaches in Corona del Mar are first viewed from the cliffs above, and they are so inviting. Little Corona in particular is a lovely little beach to take the kids because the swells are small and there are fewer undercurrents to worry about. Little Corona is predominantly a locals beach and doesn't have any stairs to get down to the beach, making it easier to access for those who are differently-abled. There is only street parking, however, and a steep incline to get down to the beach which might make it difficult for people with mobility issues. Overall, a solid choice if you're looking to feel like a local!

Table Rock Beach, 1000 Steps Beach, and Victoria Beach

These three beaches are all in Laguna and each has its own special qualities. I put them together because of their similarity of access (lots of stairs), limited parking along PCH, but mostly, their beauty.

1000 Steps Beach is the largest of the three, and it's not really 1000 steps - just 218! This beach is great for body surfing, snorkeling, SUPing (stand-up paddling), and the tide pools. It also has a sea cave at the south end of the beach!

Table Rock is another of my favorites to visit when I don't intend to do much in the water. You'll feel the excitement build as you walk down the many steps, and as the beach opens up to you, you'll know why you came here. It's just gorgeous - sandy beach, beautiful water, amazing rock outcroppings. Bring your camera!

Have your camera ready for Victoria Beach too since it may be the most famous of these three beaches thanks to its "Pirate Tower". This beach is a fun place to visit, take pictures, have a little picnic, surf, swim, and explore the tidepools. This beach has it all!

Woman gets close to the breaking waves at Victoria Beach. Photo by K. E. Bennett.

Strands Beach in Dana Point

Strands Beach is another beautiful beach that I most frequently think of as a place to walk. It could be a nice little workout if you were to do a few sets of the stairs that get you down to the beach (174 steps), or the beach is handicapped accessible with a funicular to get down to the sand. This beach can get a little skinny at high tide which limits the number of beachgoers during high tide.

5

Fabulous Shopping Destinations

Orange County has some fantastic shopping destinations, each with a little different feel as well as a huge variety of offerings.

South Coast Plaza in Costa Mesa (not quite coastal)

South Coast Plaza, the largest shopping mall in California and the fourth-largest in the United States, is truly a shopping destination. It contains 275 boutiques and is in its 55th year of operation. So many of the premium luxury brands you are looking for will be found at South Coast Plaza. It is a shopping destination that can be difficult to navigate in a single day, but if shopping is your sport, you might be able to do it! There are also many great restaurants within and very close to the mall. It is a world class shopping experience, and your friends will be envious!

Fashion Island in Newport Beach

Fashion Island in Newport Beach embodies the style and feel of coastal Orange County. It is an outdoor mall with premium luxury brands around every corner. There is a beautiful koi pond, fountains, and during the holiday season, an enormous Christmas tree. If shopping at South Coast Plaza makes you feel like you're at one of the premier big city malls in the country (and maybe beyond), Fashion Island makes you feel like you're a premier mall that overlooks the ocean in addition to having spectacular shopping options. In Southern California, where the weather is almost always nice, I prefer shopping at Fashion Island to South Coast Plaza. I'm also not a fashionista, so there's that! You can never go wrong taking a little stroll and getting a gelato - it's definitely a lovely way to spend a couple of hours.

The gigantic Christmas tree at Fashion Island delights shoppers each winter. Photo by K. E. Bennett.

Irvine Spectrum Center

Irvine Spectrum is another large and fantastic outdoor mall which is slightly inland from Newport Beach. This mall isn't as luxurious as South Coast or Fashion Island, but it still has great shops and attractions. It has a large ferris wheel and a carousel which are nice for kids and adults alike, and there is a movie theater on site. This mall is inland a bit, so it doesn't quite fall into the category of coastal Orange County, but it is a great destination, 19 miles from Newport Beach and only 10 miles from Laguna Beach.

The Irvine Spectrum is a beautiful outdoor shopping center. Photo by demxx.
https://www.flickr.com/photos/demxx/9484778342

Pacific City in Huntington Beach and Downtown Hunt-

ington Beach

Pacific City is right on Pacific Coast Highway in the heart of Huntington Beach. Many of the restaurants have outdoor seating as well as ocean views. While there is some shopping at Pacific City, I wouldn't call it a shopping destination - it's more of a lifestyle destination with some shopping. There are lots of eateries, spanning all different tastes, outdoor seating overlooking the ocean, occasional live music, and importantly, it is right next to the large resort hotels that are directly across from the ocean in Huntington Beach. Pacific City is walking distance from the pier and walking distance from the resort hotels. It's a great place to hang out if you want to be outside enjoying the beach weather.

Downtown Huntington Beach on Main Street has many more restaurants, bars, and shops. There is usually a sale going on at one of the several surf shops, there are different types of ice cream, outdoor eating, and lots of people watching. Take the time to walk down the pier while you're there. There's even a restaurant at the very end of the pier. It's quite a view!

Balboa Island

Balboa Island is another smaller shopping destination which has an idyllic feel to it. You'll want to stroll up both sides of the street to see all of the little boutiques and places to grab a snack or a meal. No trip to Balboa Island is complete without sitting outside on one of the wooden benches and enjoying a Balboa Bar or frozen banana dipped in chocolate and your choice of toppings. I always go for the nuts but the sprinkles look yummy too!

An up close view of a frozen banana, dipped in chocolate and sprinkles being eaten on the sidewalk one warm afternoon on Balboa Island. Photo by C. Ledford.

Downtown Main Streets at the Beach - Laguna, San Clemente, and Seal Beach

Laguna Beach - the downtown area is right off Main Beach and is the largest downtown area of the three. It has excellent restaurants, art galleries, boutiques, and little markets. You can never go wrong with a day trip to Laguna Beach. I have spent countless afternoons wandering the shops and countless mornings enjoying breakfast or a walk and a coffee on the boardwalk at Main Beach. In fact the cover of this book was photographed on just such a morning at Main Beach.

San Clemente - this darling little town, all grown up, was established in 1925 and marketed to home buyers as "The Spanish Village by the Sea." It has kept this charm and feel in many areas of the city including its downtown main street area, even though I still feel like it's "Carmel South." Even with that old village charm, it feels the newest and most revitalized of these three beach downtown areas. It is also the furthest to travel depending on where you're staying. The shopping here is mainly smaller boutiques.

Seal Beach - is the sleepiest of these three downtowns. While it can be bustling on a busy summer weekend, most other times the crowds are much thinner and it becomes a very relaxing and peaceful way to spend a couple of hours. Seal Beach is your pick if you don't feel like being part of a "scene" you just feel like getting out and enjoying some air and the beautiful pier. The shopping here is mainly smaller boutiques. The Irish Bars are always fun if you're feeling like a little "bit o' the Blarney".

6

Dining Out

There are so many options for dining out that it's almost impossible to choose, yet I have chosen my very favorites that would be suitable for a vacation vibe. Most are nicer, "birthday night" restaurants, and I hope you enjoy them as much as I do!

The Farmhouse at Roger's Gardens (Corona del Mar)

This is perhaps my favorite restaurant in Orange County. It is located within the Roger's Gardens nursery in Corona del Mar and serves incredibly fresh farm to table foods. Their wine list is unexpected yet fabulous and you can only eat outside. While this is a high end restaurant, there are reasonably priced offerings. The mussels and other seafood are spectacular, and they have a fantastic burger, steak, and vegetarian/vegan options. You simply can't go wrong at this restaurant - they really have it dialed in.

Outdoor patio seating at The Bungalow is intimate and welcoming, and the food is exceptional! Photo by K. E. Bennett.

BLK (Huntington Beach)

With its second floor outdoor patio overlooking the Pacific Ocean and the Huntington Beach Pier, it would be hard to find a more quintessential Huntington Beach steakhouse. BLK is known for its steak, seafood, and cocktails and it does not disappoint. The Tuna Tower is an amazing and gorgeous appetizer and their sea bass and steaks are fantastic. If you plan to be in downtown HB, this is a solid choice for good food, a great vibe, and an iconic view.

Mastro's (Newport Beach - Crystal Cove)

Mastro's has big-steakhouse energy and the menu to go with it. There is a strict dress code, and this is a place to go "see and be seen" in addition to enjoying a beautiful menu and dining experience. This is not a place I go often, but it is beloved by many and is often the birthday or anniversary choice for friends. Wear your nicest clothes and get dolled up to go have an amazing time on the patio or in one of the beautiful indoor dining areas.

Marche Moderne (Newport Beach - Crystal Cove)

Marche Moderne offers relaxed yet sophisticated fine dining. It has been around since 2007 and continues to be one of the best restaurants in Orange County. It is run by a husband and wife chef team that continue to delight their guests, and if you are a foodie or enjoy French cuisine, Marche Moderne is an excellent choice for dinner.

A Restaurant (Newport Beach - Crystal Cove)

The original location of this restaurant has been around for 90 years, and there are several locations. The Crystal Cove location is lively, cozy, warm, and spectacular - particularly during the Holidays. This just feels like a special occasion place from the moment you walk through the door. The food is excellent and the drinks are amazing, but the wine list is even more spectacular. Just be sure to bring your credit card - the one with the big limit!

Walt's Wharf (Seal Beach)

Sitting in the bar for dinner at Walt's Wharf is my favorite way to dine there. The full menu is served and there are just a few tables available in the bar area. It's possible to snag one if you're patient and/or you get there early. The bar area is surrounded with windows, so it's a lovely place to sit and watch the people walk by on Main Street. The seafood is fantastic, the bread is great, it's really a great homey-feeling restaurant with excellent food.

The Galley Cafe (breakfast and lunch only in Newport Beach)

The Galley Cafe is the only restaurant on my list that doesn't qualify as a special occasion place, but it sure does feel like a special occasion when I go there! The Galley is a tiny 1950's style diner that was established in 1957, and it maintains its old-school charm to this day. It's diner food, served diner style, by the water, and it couldn't be a nicer experience. Be prepared to wait, but I think it's worth it for the experience.

The old-school vibe is strong inside and out. I hope you enjoy this local's favorite! Photo credit @galleycafenewportbeach on instagram.com

7

Great Hikes and Walks

I'm not going to spend too much time on coastal Orange County hikes because most of it can be summed up quite succinctly - Laguna Canyon Wilderness. There are so many hikes for all different levels, and the majority have some sort of elevation gain and would best be tackled by those with a certain level of fitness. I strongly recommend looking at Alltrails.com for some of their recommendations and reviews. It's also worth noting that these hikes are all exposed to the sun with very little (if any) shade. If it's summertime, a morning hike will be the way to go.

Here are some photos from hikes I've taken in the Laguna Canyon Wilderness:

COASTAL ORANGE COUNTY CALIFORNIA TRAVEL GUIDE

The Boat Road to Bommer Ridge can be a short, 45 minute up and back, or up to 4 hours exploring the Laguna Coast Wilderness Park. Photo by M. Mulcahy.

Serrano Ridge Trail in the Laguna Coast Wilderness Park can be a longer loop - up to 7 miles. Photo by M. Mulcahy.

There are also some really nice walks along the coast. You don't need me to tell you that the beach is gorgeous, and walking down a pier or two is very enjoyable as well. There are also a couple of wetlands worth noting that have flat, and family friendly walks that you might try. On my walks in the wetlands I almost always see a Blue Heron, Snowy Egrets, Pelicans, many other types of birds, and, if I'm lucky, an Osprey!

The first wetlands is the **Newport Beach Back Bay**. This down and back walk or bike ride can be up to 8 miles, but it can also be done in bite-sized pieces. Be mindful that the walking path is also open to cars (one lane only). While there is very little traffic, you might find that a car or two travels slowly down the road.

The Back Bay wetlands walking path from the cliffs above. Photo M. Phillips.

The other wetlands is the **Bolsa Chica Ecological Reserve** which is a 1300 acre coastal estuary. It is very popular with locals who run, walk, and bird. There are so many species of birds in this wetlands area and it is one of my favorite places to go.

The rising moon shines on the water at the Bolsa Chica Ecological Reserve. An Egret and a Blue Heron hunt in the foreground. Photo by K. E. Bennett.

8

Family Friendly Experiences

Disneyland - Anaheim (not coastal)

Need I say more? I could write books about Disneyland alone! Do some research so you can have the best time possible and enjoy!

Knott's Berry Farm - Buena Park (not coastal)

Knott's Berry Farm is an amusement park that used to be a farm, and is a great alternative to Disneyland if your family has already been to Disneyland. Knott's has some great attractions and has some features that make it a great destination for the family. One of the things I appreciate most is the area that is only for younger children. Another thing that's great about Knott's is there are lots more rides than Disneyland even though it is a smaller park overall. And finally, some of the rides are really intense - much more intense than Disneyland! Knott's is also quite a bit less expensive than Disneyland, so don't overlook it if you're looking for a theme-park type adventure!

FAMILY FRIENDLY EXPERIENCES

Discovery Cube - Santa Ana (not coastal)

The Discovery Cube is an educational, hands-on, science-based kids museum. It's a favorite educational field trip for local students and the kids love it and get to experience phenomena in a real and meaningful way. It's a great choice if you want to do something completely "kid-centric" for an afternoon.

The Discovery Science Center in Santa Ana has some fun exhibits for kids. By Jason Hickey. https://commons.wikimedia.org/wiki/File:T-Rex_skeleton_at_Discovery_Science_Center.jpg

Pretend City Children's Museum - Irvine (not coastal)

The Pretend City Children's Museum is for children aged Pre-K

- 2nd grade and encourages children to get involved in a hand's-on way in the workings of a pretend city. There are roles to play from farmer to doctor and dental hygienist to UPS driver. All the while, children are developing vocabulary, fine motor skills, creativity, problem-solving, and cooperation! All while having fun! Take your kiddos for a fun couple of hours of play that is just their size and speed!

Balboa Fun Zone - Newport Peninsula

Welcome to a slice of yesterday, with old-style arcade games, a ferris wheel, a couple of other boardwalk attractions, and old style foods that will give you a slice of Americana all by the ocean! This is right next to the Balboa Ferry entrance, so hop aboard and cross the water to Balboa Island!

The Balboa Fun Zone is right on the water at one end of the ferry. https://commons.wikimedia.org/wiki/File:Fun_ ZonePhoto_D_Ramey_Logan.jpg By Don Ramey Logan

FAMILY FRIENDLY EXPERIENCES

For the Nature-Lovers:

Whale Watching - Dana Point

Being that Southern California is along the whale migration route, there are lots of opportunities to see migrating whales. Of course that means we don't always see whales, but there are lots of whale sightings in Southern California. This summer there were tons of blue whales, I saw a fin whale this summer, and even orcas have made an appearance! Regardless of whether or not you see a whale, these trips are very enjoyable, give you a nice look at the coastline and the deep water, and are fun for all ages! Get out there!

Dana Point Ocean Institute, Tide Pools, and Sea Cave - Dana Point

There are three great ocean-related activities in Dana Point. The Ocean Institute is a great place for kids and adults to learn all about the ocean, its inhabitants, and how we can be better stewards of such a majestic body of water. The Tide Pools and Sea Cave are best visited during low tide and the walk there can be quite rocky. It's best to wear sturdy shoes if you choose to venture down the beach and immerse yourself in the beautiful surroundings.

Tanaka Farms - Irvine (not coastal)

Tanaka Farms is a real working family owned 30-acre farm in the heart of Irvine that provides "you-pick' events, tours and educational opportunities. It is so fun to pick your own strawberries or vegetables (season dependent) and enjoy learning about what a real working farm is like. Great for the kids or fun for a daytime date event. Check out their website for tour times, reservations, and picking opportunities.

Sherman Library and Gardens - Corona del Mar

Sherman Library and Gardens is a nationally renowned botanical garden and has beautiful garden exhibits throughout its grounds with a small library. There are tropical, desert, herb, and succulent exhibits, fountains, a garden-centric gift shop, and a beautiful lunch venue adjacent to the gardens. At times there is live music as well. This is a beautiful location that gives a lot and doesn't expect a lot in return. The entry fee is nominal, and the entire garden can be walked in an hour if you are walking with purpose. A more leisurely stroll and time spent more thoroughly enjoying the exhibits might take a couple of hours. The foliage is truly amazing - check it out if time permits!

FAMILY FRIENDLY EXPERIENCES

The gardens are lovely any time of year, but this is quite a display of flowers! https://www.flickr.com/photos/131880272@N06/48273730526 Photo by cultivar413

9

Cultural Experiences

If you're looking for the big name museum and cultural experiences, it's best to go to Los Angeles and visit the Los Angeles County Museum of Art, The Broad Museum, The Getty, or even the Griffith Observatory. For theater and concerts that might include the Hollywood Bowl, the Pantages or the Ahmanson Theater, or the Disney Concert Hall. All of these, among many others, are amazing experiences that would constitute three quarters of a day or a whole day's adventure if traveling from Orange County. Although coastal Orange County doesn't have the powerhouse museums and culturals sites that are found in Los Angeles, there is a lot of local culture - some of it world renowned, and some of it quirky local culture. Here's a peek at my favorites:

Segerstrom Center For the Arts - Costa Mesa (not quite coastal)

Segerstrom is where I go to see theater, ballet and fine art concerts like jazz and classical. It's a beautiful venue which has both a theater, concert hall, and outdoor patio for events. The artists are world class, and I've seen shows like Jersey Boys, Six, Les Miserables, the Russian Ballet, an Abba tribute band, classical music concerts, and other great shows! Check out their website while you're planning your trip to see if there's anything you want to see while you're in town.

The beautifully designed Segerstrom Concert Hall. Photo by Tracie Hall.
https://www.flickr.com/photos/twobears2/15986443975

Mission San Juan Capistrano - San Juan Capistrano (not quite coastal)

San Juan Capistrano's downtown area, while just a touch inland from Dana Point beaches, is one of my favorite places to visit, dine, and walk. Mission San Juan Capistrano is 7th of 21 historic missions built statewide by the spanish padres, and is home site of the historic legend of the swallows returning to Capistrano in March every year. The missions of California are always interesting to visit and take a trip back in time to see what life was like for these self-sufficient communities. The restaurant's in the area are fantastic, with Trevor's at the Tracks, and the San Juan Capistrano Winery being among my favorites. The Swallows Inn is a great local spot for live music and cocktails.

The San Juan Capistrano Mission.
https://commons.wikimedia.org/wiki/File:2019_Mission_ San_Juan_Capistrano_arcade_and_domes_of_the_Mission_ Basilica_San_Juan_Capistrano.jpg

Bowers Museum - Santa Ana - (not coastal)

The Bowers Museum is in the heart of Orange County, and while not as prestigious or well known as some of the museums in LA, nevertheless exhibits some of the world's finest art and artifacts. They partner with museums around the world and bring world class fine art exhibits to Orange County. The Bower's has been voted best museum in Orange County 29 years in a row by the Orange County Register Readers. Exhibits have included China's Terracotta Warriors, the Mummies Exhibit, California Art, and Gemstone/Jewelry Exhibits. If you are interested in fine art and enjoy museums, this smaller museum, close to the coast is a great choice.

Pageant of the Master's - Laguna Beach - (seasonal)

Pageant of the Masters is a seasonal show that features fine art tableaus which are created on a full-sized stage with backdrops and actors. The Pageant of the Masters artists make their tableau art looks exactly like the original fine art piece to the amazement of the audience! It is a really fun experience to sit outdoors in the amphitheater on a summer night and witness their expertise in this optical illusion. Multiple, thematic pieces of art are replicated, and there is a segment during which they deconstruct the tableau so you can see how it comes together. Magical!

Sawdust Art Festival - Laguna Beach - (seasonal)

The Sawdust Festival is a summer and winter outdoor festival where local artists display their work for sale. Many times there is live music, and the exhibits run from finer art to crafts, handmade greeting cards, jewelry, and other creative endeavors that are so enjoyable to browse and shop. There are also demonstration booths as well as art classes during the non-festival months where locals and visitors can learn from the exhibiting artists.

Laguna Beach Art Walk - Laguna Beach (first Thursdays)

The Laguna Beach Art Walk is a locals favorite where art galleries throughout Laguna open their galleries from 6 - 9 pm in the evening and encourage people to enjoy the exhibits. Some galleries offer wine or cheese, or other beverages, but I wouldn't plan on making it dinner. Take your time to enjoy the galleries and take in the art - maybe you'll even be inspired to purchase something, but it's certainly not required!

Balboa Island Museum and Historical Society - Newport Beach

If you're interested in the local history of Newport Beach and Balboa Island, this is the place for you. The museum is right by the Balboa Ferry and Fun Zone and would make a nice cultural addition to a trip to the Balboa Island area. The museum is housed in the original building, built in 1927. You'll love learning about the local iconic spots and their history!

Surf Museums - Huntington Beach and San Clemente

There are two surf museums in Orange County for those who really love surfing or love surf culture. They are both small museums, but they pack in a lot of opportunities to learn about the history of surfing. Enjoy!

10

Non-Hiking Adventures

Paddleboard or Kayak - Dana Point Harbor, Newport Harbor, Huntington Harbour

Paddleboarding and kayaking are two fun activities that get you out on the water and having lots of fun in the sun as well as getting a little exercise. My personal favorite location to paddleboard is Dana Point Harbor because the water is so clear and you can see the fish swimming in the water below you! I love that! Any of the locations is good for paddleboarding or kayaking as both sports lend themselves to harbors where the waters are smoother and calmer. I would like to mention that although we're looking for fun in the sun and it seems like the afternoon would be the perfect time to do these activities, in most cases you will have a better experience in the morning because the wind will not have picked up yet. I have found myself on more than one occasion, stuck on the rocks, or having a difficult time making any headway on my paddleboard or in my kayak because the winds were so strong. Lesson learned - I go in the morning now! Avoid the wind - go out in the morning, and you'll have more fun!

Paddleboarding and kayaking in Huntington Harbour. Photo by K. E. Bennett.

Boating - Dana Point, Newport Harbor, Huntington Harbour

Rent an electric Duffy boat and put-put around the harbor with a little wine and cheese. Captaining the boats is not difficult and most rental places will help you get into your slip on the return trip easily since docking the boat is the hardest part! You can do it and you'll have fun!

Sailing is a lot of fun but can be intimidating if you don't know how. Check out locations in the area where you can get someone to go with you and sail a small, single-sail or two-sailed boat, with help, so you can see just how fun it is to corral the wind and make it move your boat the way you want it to! I've done this in Dana Point with my young daughter and a friend and we had a blast!

Freedom Boat Club, and other subscription boating companies, have boats in several harbors for you to take out if you are a member.

View of the harbor and the snow-capped mountains from a duffy boat. Photo by K. E. Bennett.

Surfing - so many choices dependent on your skill level

Learning to surf can take anywhere from two hours to a month. If you want to learn to surf on your vacation and be successful, you will need to get hooked up with some lessons and dedicate more than one session in the water. Surfing isn't a highly demanding sport, however, if your upper body isn't trained, paddling to catch waves will get pretty tiring. Enjoy some lessons at many of the beaches and "catch a wave"!

Kite Surfing - Sunset Beach, Huntington Beach

Kite surfing is an extreme sport that requires some lessons and experience. If you believe the internet, it takes between 10 and 20 hours of training to get going which translates to 3-5 days of lessons. If that's one of your goals and your primary objective, it sure seems doable in a week-long vacation in Southern California! The kite-surfing is great at several OC beaches, and I most often see them kite surfing in Sunset Beach and Huntington Beach north of the pier due to the favorable wind conditions. If you're fit and have wanted to try it - educate yourself then go for it!!

Bike Ride at the Beach - Newport Beach or Huntington Beach

Bike riding on the strand at the beach is a quintessential beach holiday activity. I try to do it weekly as a local!! You can choose to rent regular beach cruisers or electric bikes. I would let your fitness and the wind be your guide. The rides aren't long even if you do them tip to tail, so a beach cruiser is plenty of bike if you have a decent level of fitness. If the wind is blowing, if your fitness isn't what it used to be, or if you choose to ride all the way from Huntington Beach to Newport Beach and back, you may want an electric bike. If you're just interested in a little ride to get out, enjoy the sunshine, and maybe have a cocktail or a bite to eat, I recommend the strand in Newport. If you are more interested in riding and less interested in the food/drink aspect of the experience, Huntington Beach might be a better choice for you. Enjoy!

NON-HIKING ADVENTURES

Biking on the Newport Beach bike path. Photo J. Karzak

Catalina Island Day Trip - Catalina Island with boats leaving from Dana Point, Newport, and Long Beach

A day trip to Catalina island is a really fun day! You get to spend time on the ocean on the passages over and back, explore the island via golf cart or e-bike, have some "buffalo milk"- a delicious locally famous cocktail, shop, enjoy the beach, dine, and generally enjoy the beautiful scenery and weather. Catalina is a fun trip but it really is an all day trip. Do some investigations and see if it is for you and/or your family.

View of Catalina at sunset from Huntington Beach. The allure of Catalina is endless. No matter how many times I go, I want to travel across the sea again to visit that pretty little island. Photo by K. E. Bennett

Angels Baseball Game - Anaheim Stadium

NON-HIKING ADVENTURES

If you're a baseball fan and the Angels are in town, taking in a baseball game is a great way to spend an afternoon or evening. Angels stadium is relatively easy to get in and out of. I recently attended a game and had an amazing time. The stadium is friendly and easy to navigate. For the ladies, please remember your tiny bags or clear purses!

The seats don't get much better than this, but regardless, a day at the ballpark is always a blast. Photo by K. E. Bennett.

Gondola Rides - Newport Harbor

Take a ride in an old Venetian-style gondola with a gondolier for a guide through Newport Harbor. There are so many options to suit your taste and budget, but as of this writing, the least expensive option for a one-hour cruise for two was $165, and full dinner service ranged as high as $500 and up. Lots to choose from and gondolas can take up to six passengers with an additional charge per person above two passengers. I've done this in Venice, Italy but not Newport Beach. It was a blast and I know it would be amazing in Newport Beach as well - writing this is making me want to go! There are other options in other harbors as well, if that is your preference.

Spa Days - Pelican Hill, Montage, Surf and Sand

Having a spa day or a spa experience at any of these three hotels is sure to be an exceptional experience. According to Modern Luxury Riviera Orange County, these are three of the nicest spa experiences in the area. If you're looking for a high end spa experience, these three places are my recommendation as well. I love to frequent these hotels for lunch (Pelican Hill), cocktails and a raging fire in the winter (Montage), and oceanfront dining (Surf and Sand). Or do them all in one day!

NON-HIKING ADVENTURES

View from the Montage lobby bar during the Holiday Season.
Photo by K. E. Bennett.

11

Outdoor Bars With A View

One of my favorite ways to enjoy Orange County is outdoors with a view. It's a tough way to live but somebody's gotta do it - and it looks like it's your turn too!

Duke's or Sandy's - Huntington Beach Pier

There is very little that is more iconic than the Huntington Beach Pier area. Sandy's restaurant has a bit of an edge for me over Duke's for the view because their patio is directly on the strand at the beach. You can look directly out onto the beach, see the volleyball players, the skaters and bicyclists cruising by, and the pier and ocean as well. I love this place when I'm at the pier.

Duke's is directly upstairs from Sandy's and has gorgeous views of exactly the same thing as Sandy's, but it's available from the dining room only. Never fear, Duke's has a lovely patio that sits directly across from the plaza that is the entrance to the pier.

You can watch street performers, beach-goers, protesters, and proselytizers from your shaded vantage point, all with a nice menu from Duke's. I tend to go to Duke's more often because I feel like I get to see more people, but if you're really set on being next to the sand, go for Sandy's.

Winter view from Sandy's Restaurant in Huntington Beach. Photo by K. E. Bennett

Tanner's Treehouse - Pasea Hotel in Huntington Beach

Tanner's is a beautiful outdoor, second floor bar with an expansive view of the water and the beach. During the day, the outdoor seating is great for catching some sun, or shading yourself with an umbrella, and at night, the music and dancing are a ton of fun! Don't miss the swings as you're walking toward the restrooms! The treehouse has a whimsical theme that is well done, with an upscale, festive vibe. You can walk to Tanner's from Pacific City, so while you're visiting, stop by the Treehouse to relax and take in even more of the beautiful coastline. The couch and fire pit area is a lovely respite after a long day of sightseeing or shopping.

Offshore 9 Rooftop Lounge - Hilton Hotel in Huntington Beach

This lounge is on the 9th floor of the HIlton Hotel overlooking Pacific Coast Highway, the sand, and the water in Huntington Beach. The view is expansive and is the main reason to come here. If you're staying in the hotel, definitely make a stop, and if you're looking for a fantastic view of the pier and beach, this is a great place to find it. The drinks here are good but a little on the expensive side - as you might expect from a hotel bar - but the view and the photos you'll get from this spot make it worth it. If you're going during the summer, the weather should be perfect. At any other time, the offshore breeze can make it quite cool, even with the fire pits - bring a sweater.

The Bungalow - Pacific City, Huntington Beach

The Bungalow is a chain of restaurants, but this particular location is a lounge (not a restaurant) known for its drinks and atmosphere. Food can be ordered from the Bear Flag restaurant directly below it. Multiple rooms throughout give you the ability to choose a spot that's just right for you. Leather couches, low tables, dark walls, a pool table in one of the rooms, and the outside deck, which is the reason for it being on this list. I think this outside deck has such a friendly vibe, yet it's upscale like you're on vacation. To me, it is one of the nicest outdoor bars by the ocean. The crowd is typically young, and be aware that this is one of the late night spots in Huntington Beach that frequently has a line to get in.

The Rooftop Lounge - La Casa del Camino Hotel in Laguna Beach

This rooftop lounge is one of my very favorites in Orange County. It has been around for years and offers an exceptional happy hour featuring California casual cuisine and spectacular sunsets. If you're spending time in Laguna while you're in town, a trip to this bar is worth the effort, and it will yield memories that will last a lifetime. I've been to this bar a handful of times, and I remember each and every time. And while it's open during the day, and it's always lovely, I find that the changing light of sunset lends a magical quality that makes it even more memorable. Enjoy.

15FiftyFive - Surf and Sand Resort in Laguna Beach

15FiftyFive is an outdoor bar, adjacent to the lobby of the Surf and Sand Resort and has a beautiful view of the ocean. This is the outdoor version of Surf and Sand restaurant/bar offerings. I also really enjoy Splashes, which is indoors, but with expansive windows that make it feel like the ocean is directly outside the window. Whichever you choose, you will have a memorable experience enjoying some of the most breathtaking views Laguna has to offer.

Sol - Newport Beach

Sol has excellent tacos and margaritas, and if you're looking for a relaxed spot to eat, you can find it at the bar or on the outdoor patio looking over the marina. While this isn't an expansive view of the ocean, it's still a beautiful spot to sit, watch the water, the boats, and the paddle-boarders pass by. Delicious food and delicious drinks make this a memorable spot and one of my favorites.

Sea Legs at the Beach - Huntington Beach

Sea Legs is a beach bar that is directly on the sand. You can get there by bicycle, by walking down the bike path, or by parking in one of the state parking lots along Pacific Coast Highway. SeaLegs has cover bands on the weekends and a "Breakfast with the Beatles" brunch with a Beatles cover band. You can have your toes in the sand while you eat, drink, and enjoy being on the beach listening to live music.

Green Cheek Beer Company - Sunset Beach

Green Cheek is a very casual brewery with delicious beers and flavorful bites to eat. If you go upstairs, you will find a lovely roof deck with umbrellas and sliver of a view of the Pacific Ocean through the houses across the street. This isn't really a place you come for the view - it's more of a place to just unwind after a day at the beach, or stop by on your bike ride up and down the coast. Sit outside in the sun or under an umbrella, order food and drink either upstairs or downstairs, and relax and unwind. Don't forget to try the tater tots - they're pretty great!!

A quiet Monday at Green Cheek's rooftop bar with a view and the best tater tots around. Photo by K. E. Bennett

12

Conclusion

Thank you for allowing me to take you on a tour through some of my favorite spots in coastal Orange County. I love to go back to these places again and again, and I hope that after you've visited some of them you feel the same.

If you've found this book helpful, I'd be really appreciative if you left a favorable review for the book on Amazon!

13

Resources

Balboa Island Museum – Museum and Historical Society Newport Beach. (n.d.). https://www.balboaislandmuseum.org/

Bolsa Chica Ecological Reserve. (n.d.). https://wildlife.ca.gov/Lands/Places-to-Visit/Bolsa-Chica-ER

Bryce, E., & Bryce, E. (2023, September 13). 69 fun things to do in Orange County, California - TourScanner. *TourScanner*. https://tourscanner.com/blog/fun-things-to-do-in-orange-county/

Chrusciel, B. (2022, November 8). 27 top things to do in Orange County, California. *US News & World Report*. https://travel.usnews.com/features/top-things-to-do-in-orange-county-california

Enjoy OC. (2023, September 21). *Your guide to Orange County & Southern California | Enjoy OC*. https://enjoyorangecounty.c

om/

Fashion Island - Shopping, dining and entertainment | Newport Beach. (n.d.). Fashion Island. https://www.fashionisland.com/

Field trips - Pretend City. (2023, September 28). Pretend City. https://www.pretendcity.org/field-trips/

McFadden, M. (2023). 41 Best & Fun Things to do in Orange County, California. The Atlas Heart. https://theatlasheart.com/things-to-do-in-orange-county/

Mission San Juan Capistrano - Mission San Juan Capistrano. (2023, September 26). Mission San Juan Capistrano. https://www.missionsjc.com/

orange county california climate - Google Search. (n.d.). https://www.google.com/search?q=orange+county+california+climate&rlz=1C5CHFA_enUS858US871&oq=orange+county+california+climate+&gs_lcrp=EgZjaHJvbWUyBggAEEUYOTIHCAEQABiABDIICAIQABgWGB4yCAgDEAAYFhgeMgoIBBAAGIYDGIoFMgoIBRAAGIYDGIoFMgoIBhAAGIYDGIoF0gEJMjI2OTlqMWo3qAIAsAIA&sourceid=chrome&ie=UTF-8

Orange County's Finest. (n.d.). Bowers Museum. https://www.bowers.org/

Sherman Library and Gardens – Discover. Learn. Engage. (n.d.). https://thesherman.org/

RESOURCES

South Coast Plaza. (n.d.). https://www.southcoastplaza.com/

The history of San Clemente, California. (n.d.). http://www.sanclementerealestate.com/the-history-of-san-clemente-california.php

Thousand Steps Beach | Visit Laguna Beach. (n.d.). Visit Laguna Beach. https://www.visitlagunabeach.com/things-to-do/beaches/thousand-steps/

Visit Dana Point. (2022, November 9). *Doheny State Beach | Doheny SB | Visit Dana Point.* https://visitdanapoint.com/what-to-do/doheny-state-beach/

Visit Newport Beach. (2023a, June 27). *Little Corona del Mar Beach | Little Corona Beach & Tidepools.* https://www.visitnewportbeach.com/beaches-and-parks/little-corona-del-mar-beach/

Visit Newport Beach. (2023b, June 27). *The Wedge in Newport Beach | Sunsets & surfing.* https://www.visitnewportbeach.com/beaches-and-parks/the-wedge/

About the Author

K. E. Bennett is a Southern California native residing in Huntington Beach. She is passionate about contributing to society by sharing her knowledge and experience. Ms. Bennett has a Bachelor's Degree, an M.B.A., and a wealth of experience in both the private and public sector. Her personal interests include healthy living, being active, and spending time with friends and family.

Made in the USA
Las Vegas, NV
05 November 2023